DENIS WAITLEY'S
◆ ◆ ◆

Little Green Book of

INSPIRATION

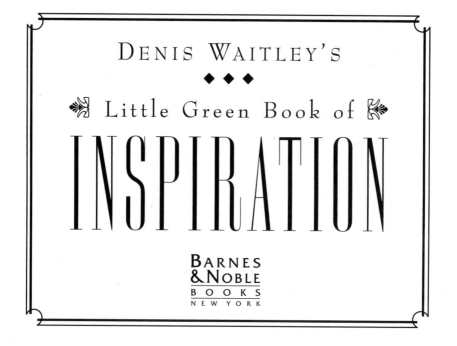

Denis Waitley's

♦ ♦ ♦

❧ Little Green Book of ❧

INSPIRATION

BARNES
&NOBLE
B O O K S
NEW YORK

This edition published by Barnes & Noble, Inc.
by arrangement with Nightingale-Conant Corp.

1995 © Nightingale-Conant Corporation

ISBN 1-56619-960-3

Book design by Rocket Design, James Sarfati

Printed and bound in the United States of America

2 4 6 8 10 M 9 7 5 3 1

About the Author

D r. Denis Waitley is one of the world's most respected authorities on personal excellence and high-level achievement. His passion has generated twelve books on self-management, audiotapes translated into fourteen languages, and countless invitations to deliver keynote addresses. In fact, Dr. Waitley was recently inducted into the International Speaker's Hall of Fame.

Dr. Waitley has conducted simulation and stress-management seminars for the *Apollo* astronauts, studied and counseled U.S. POW's returning from Vietnam, served as president of the International Society for Advanced Education, and was the founding director of both the National Council on Self-Esteem and the President's Council on Vocational Education. Most recently, Dr. Waitley can be found conducting no less than 150 seminars a year across the nation.

Dr. Waitley's best-selling titles include *The Psychology of Winning* and *The Seeds of Greatness*. His latest book is *Empires of the Mind*.

DENIS WAITLEY QUOTATIONS

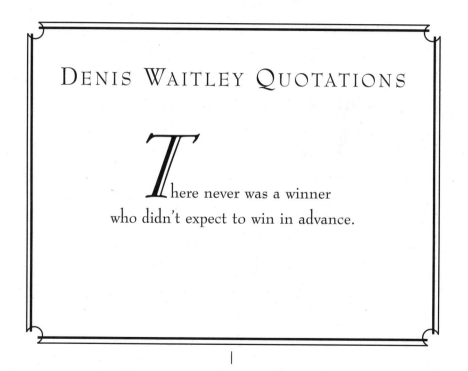

*There never was a winner
who didn't expect to win in advance.*

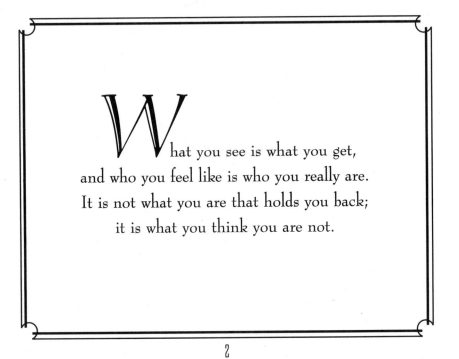

What you see is what you get,
and who you feel like is who you really are.
It is not what you are that holds you back;
it is what you think you are not.

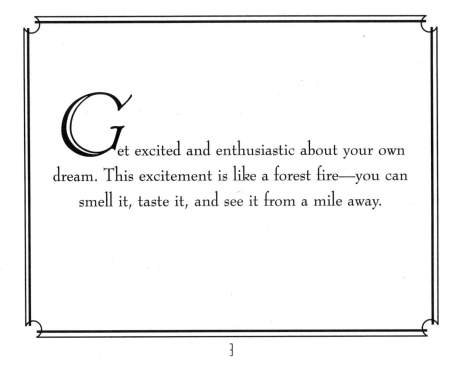

Get excited and enthusiastic about your own dream. This excitement is like a forest fire—you can smell it, taste it, and see it from a mile away.

*L*osers take chances; winners make choices.

*L*osers fix the blame;
winners fix what caused the problem.

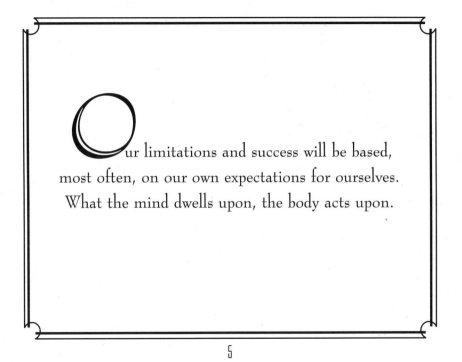

Our limitations and success will be based, most often, on our own expectations for ourselves. What the mind dwells upon, the body acts upon.

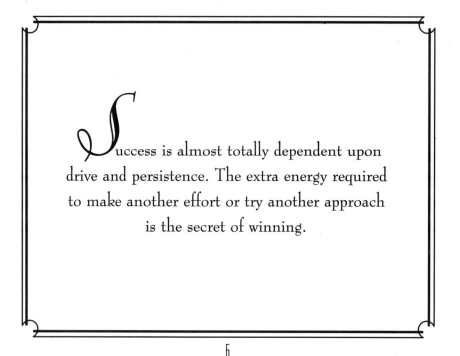

*S*uccess is almost totally dependent upon drive and persistence. The extra energy required to make another effort or try another approach is the secret of winning.

*P*ositive self-direction is the action plan
that all winners in life use to turn
imagination into reality, fantasy into fact,
and dreams into actual goals.

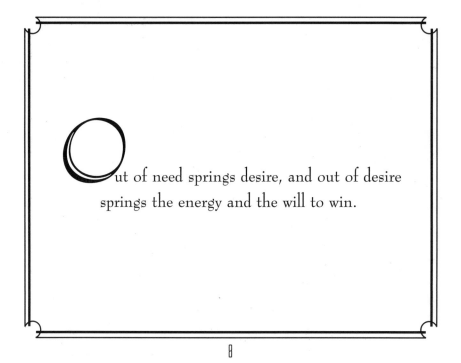

Out of need springs desire, and out of desire springs the energy and the will to win.

W inners are people with a definite
purpose in life.

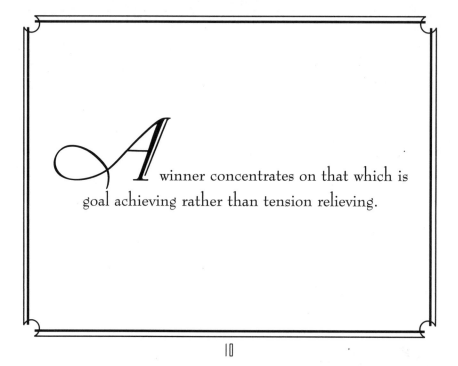

A winner concentrates on that which is goal achieving rather than tension relieving.

*L*osers make promises they often break.
Winners make commitments they always keep.

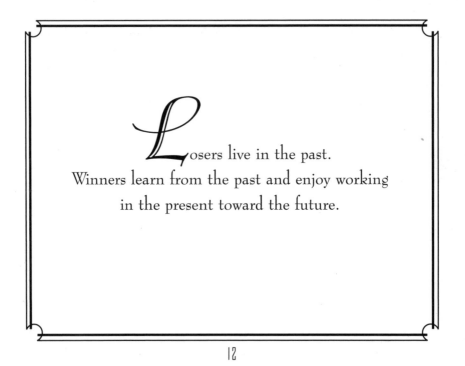

*L*osers live in the past.
Winners learn from the past and enjoy working
in the present toward the future.

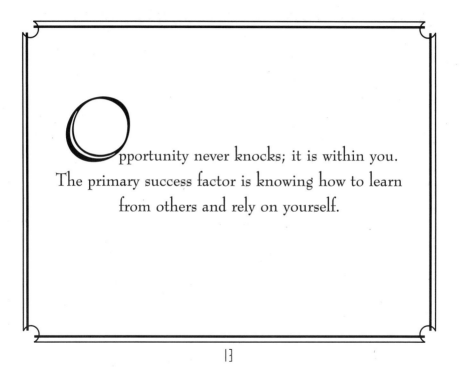

Opportunity never knocks; it is within you.
The primary success factor is knowing how to learn
from others and rely on yourself.

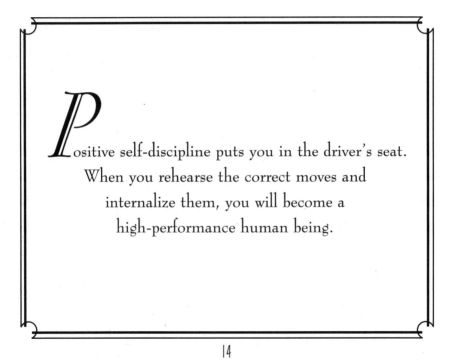

*P*ositive self-discipline puts you in the driver's seat. When you rehearse the correct moves and internalize them, you will become a high-performance human being.

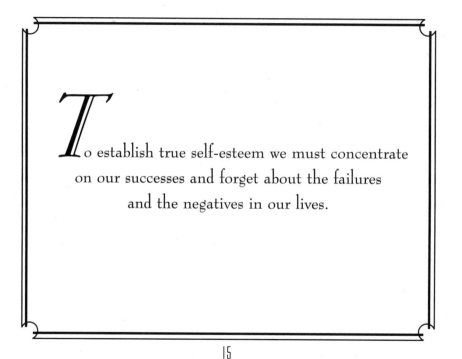

*T*o establish true self-esteem we must concentrate
on our successes and forget about the failures
and the negatives in our lives.

Since the perfect human being has not been discovered, we all need to live with our hang-ups and our idiosyncrasies until they can be ironed out. One of the most important qualities in successful, dynamic living is that of self-acceptance.

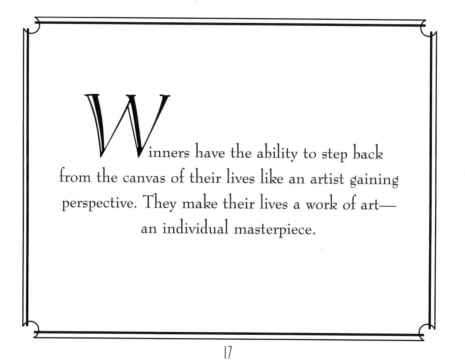

Winners have the ability to step back
from the canvas of their lives like an artist gaining
perspective. They make their lives a work of art—
an individual masterpiece.

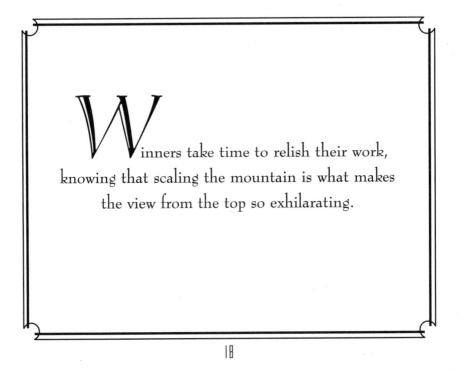

Winners take time to relish their work,
knowing that scaling the mountain is what makes
the view from the top so exhilarating.

*T*he winners in life treat their body as if it were a magnificent spacecraft that gives them the finest transportation and endurance for their lives.

*L*earn how to grow out of yourself
and into the world of others: Plant a shade tree
under which you know you will never sit. Set some
goals that may benefit your children or an orphanage
or the employees of your company or future
generations or your own city, fifty years from now.

A smile is the light in your window that tells others that there is a caring, sharing person inside.

S ince you usually get what you expect in life, expect the best for yourself.

*T*hrive on risk as a part of life.

A dream is your creative vision for your life in the future.

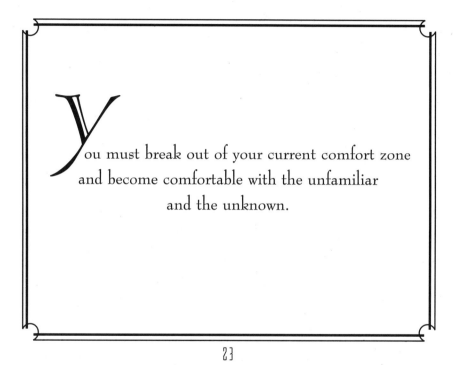

You must break out of your current comfort zone
and become comfortable with the unfamiliar
and the unknown.

*M*ake certain that your goals
are not measured in comparison with others.

*P*ersonal satisfaction is the most important
ingredient of success.

Goals are like stepping-stones to the stars.
They should never be used to put a ceiling or a limit
on achievement.

*L*ife is not acountable to us....
We are accountable to life.

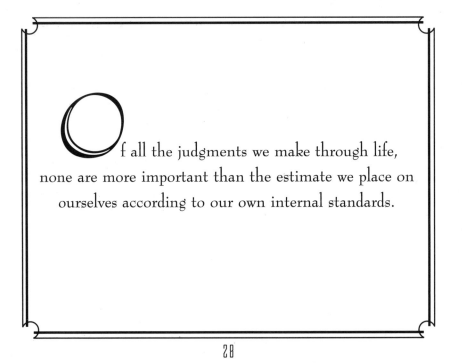

Of all the judgments we make through life, none are more important than the estimate we place on ourselves according to our own internal standards.

*D*well on the reward, and you move toward it.
Dwell on the penalty, and you move away
from the reward.

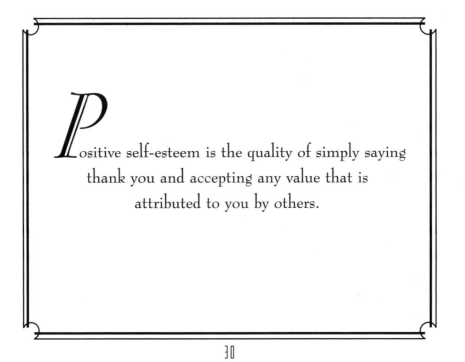

*P*ositive self-esteem is the quality of simply saying
thank you and accepting any value that is
attributed to you by others.

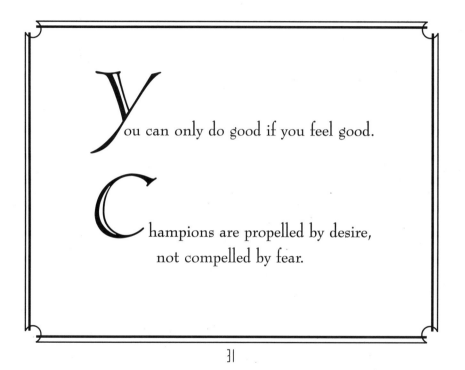

*Y*ou can only do good if you feel good.

*C*hampions are propelled by desire,
not compelled by fear.

*P*erfection is devastated by failure, while excellence learns from failure.

*E*xpect the best, plan for the worst, and prepare to be surprised.

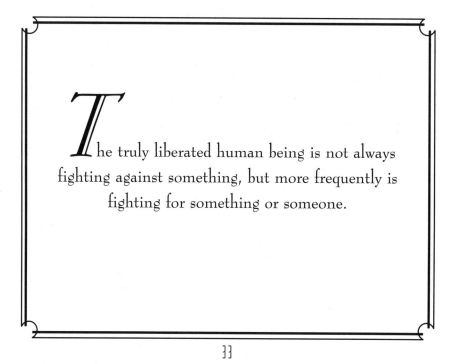

*T*he truly liberated human being is not always
fighting against something, but more frequently is
fighting for something or someone.

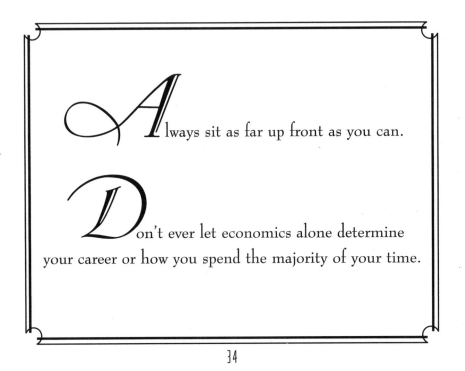

*A*lways sit as far up front as you can.

*D*on't ever let economics alone determine your career or how you spend the majority of your time.

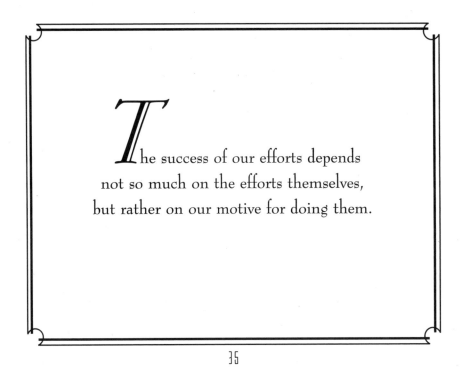

The success of our efforts depends
not so much on the efforts themselves,
but rather on our motive for doing them.

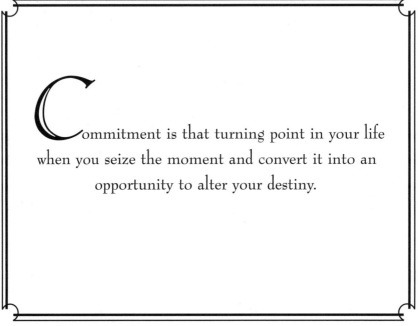

Commitment is that turning point in your life
when you seize the moment and convert it into an
opportunity to alter your destiny.

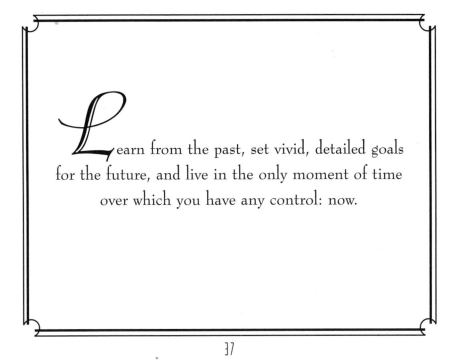

*L*earn from the past, set vivid, detailed goals for the future, and live in the only moment of time over which you have any control: now.

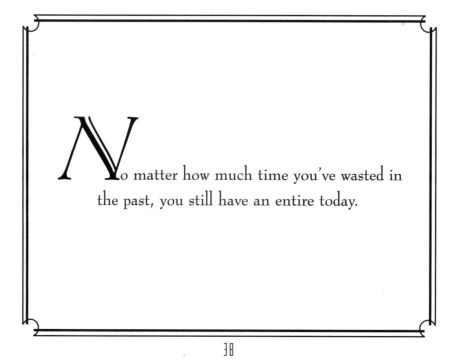

No matter how much time you've wasted in the past, you still have an entire today.

*M*istakes are painful when they happen,
but years later a collection of mistakes is
what is called experience.

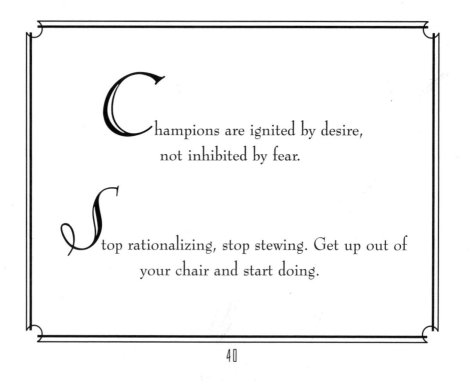

Champions are ignited by desire,
not inhibited by fear.

Stop rationalizing, stop stewing. Get up out of
your chair and start doing.

*D*on't be a time manager, be a priority manager. Cut your major goals into bite-sized pieces. Each small priority or requirement on the way to the ultimate goal becomes a minigoal in itself.

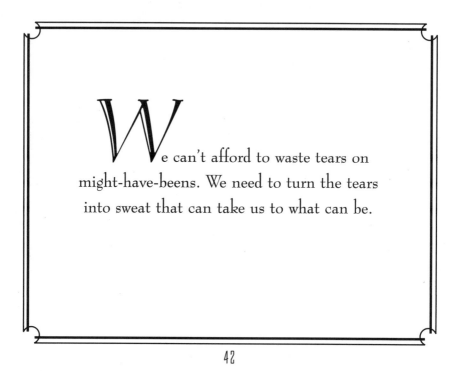

We can't afford to waste tears on might-have-beens. We need to turn the tears into sweat that can take us to what can be.

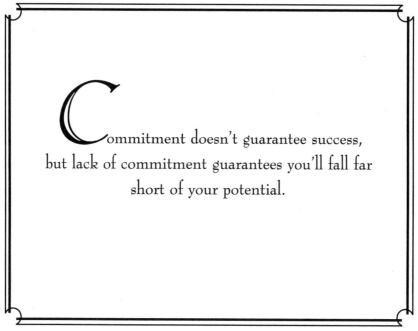

Commitment doesn't guarantee success,
but lack of commitment guarantees you'll fall far
short of your potential.

*N*ever become so much of an expert that you stop gaining expertise. View life as a continuous learning experience.

There are no mistakes or failures, only lessons.

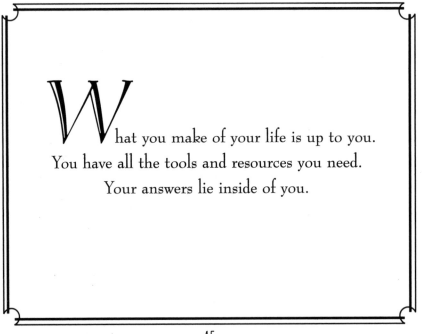

What you make of your life is up to you.
You have all the tools and resources you need.
Your answers lie inside of you.

*T*he earlier you recognize the value of your being, the more you will invest in your knowledge, skills, and performance. Performance is only a reflection of internal worth—not the measure of it.

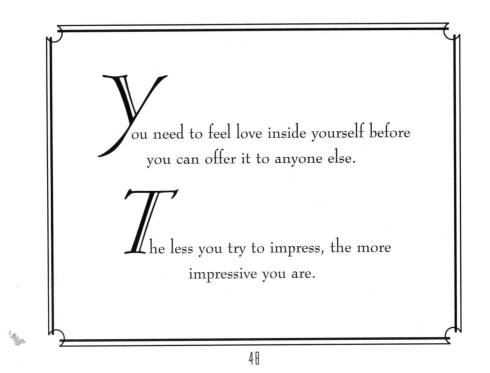

You need to feel love inside yourself before you can offer it to anyone else.

The less you try to impress, the more impressive you are.

The most important conversations, briefings, meetings, and lectures you will ever have will be those you hold with yourself in the privacy of your own mind.

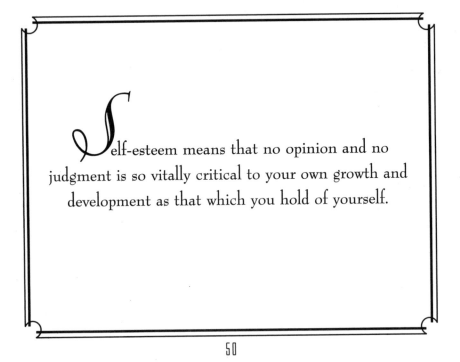

$\mathcal{S}$elf-esteem means that no opinion and no judgment is so vitally critical to your own growth and development as that which you hold of yourself.

Champions never brag, never shout, never have to go to extremes to build themselves up for others or put others down. They let their actions, deeds, and results speak for them.

$\mathcal{B}$e a role model not a critic. Don't tell your children, your peers, or your subordinates what to do—show them. And when the lesson is over, keep showing them by demonstrating that your actions are part of your character, not part of their curriculum.

A life lived with integrity—even if it lacks the trappings of fame and fortune—is a shining star in whose light others may follow in the years to come.

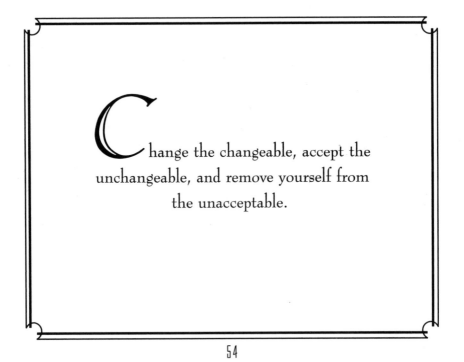

Change the changeable, accept the unchangeable, and remove yourself from the unacceptable.

*L*asting change is possible only when the need for change is both understood and internalized.

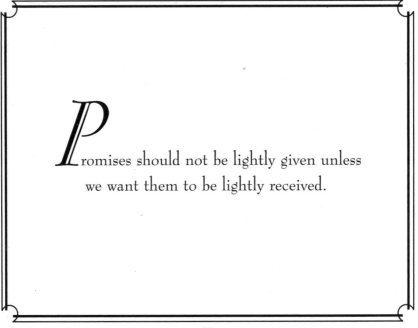

*P*romises should not be lightly given unless
we want them to be lightly received.

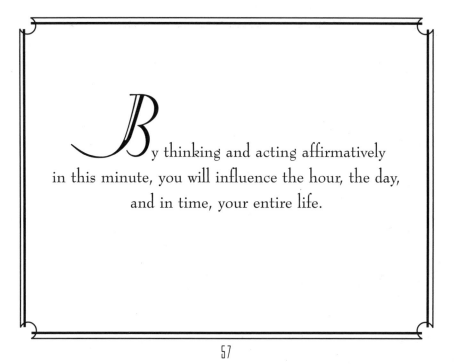

*B*y thinking and acting affirmatively in this minute, you will influence the hour, the day, and in time, your entire life.

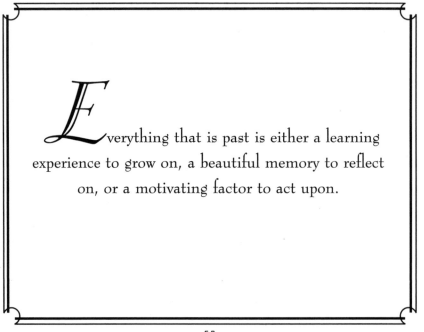

*E*verything that is past is either a learning experience to grow on, a beautiful memory to reflect on, or a motivating factor to act upon.

Since the mind can't distinguish between a real experience and one that is repeatedly and vividly imagined, in a very real sense we are the scriptwriter, main character, and director of either a victorious life story or a laborious soap opera. It all depends on the kind of message we give ourselves before, during, and after our daily performance.

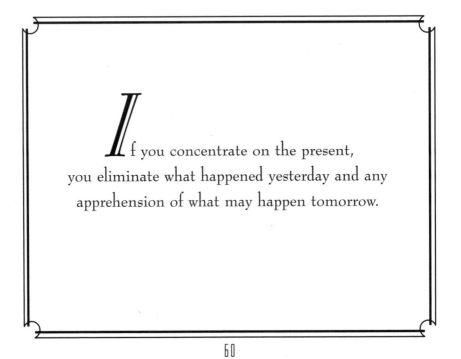

*I*f you concentrate on the present,
you eliminate what happened yesterday and any
apprehension of what may happen tomorrow.

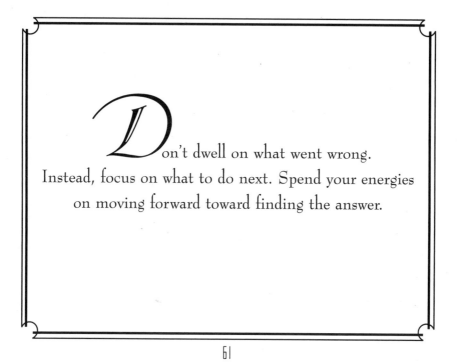

*D*on't dwell on what went wrong.
Instead, focus on what to do next. Spend your energies
on moving forward toward finding the answer.

*I*f you focus your attention strictly on your own needs, you will grow weaker and compound your needs. But if you focus your attention on something outside of yourself, you will grow stronger and feel better.

A passion for life is one of the most attractive qualities in a human being. If you want a teammate or a life mate who loves to be around you, all you need to do is love to be around.

*T*he majority of people consider their work a means to an end. People who work for money only come to the end faster than people who are involved in their life's purpose every day.

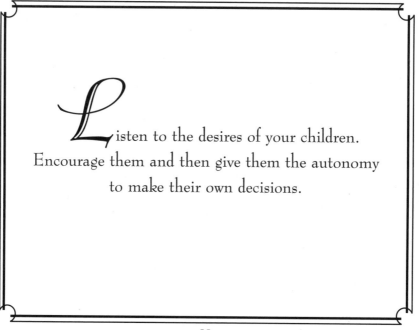

*L*isten to the desires of your children.
Encourage them and then give them the autonomy
to make their own decisions.

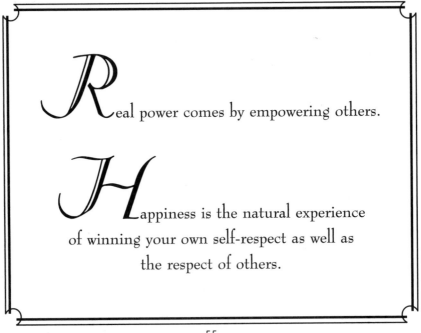

$\mathcal{R}$eal power comes by empowering others.

$\mathcal{H}$appiness is the natural experience
of winning your own self-respect as well as
the respect of others.

*T*hat which you create in beauty and goodness and truth lives on for all time to come. Don't spend your life accumulating material objects that will only turn to dust and ashes.

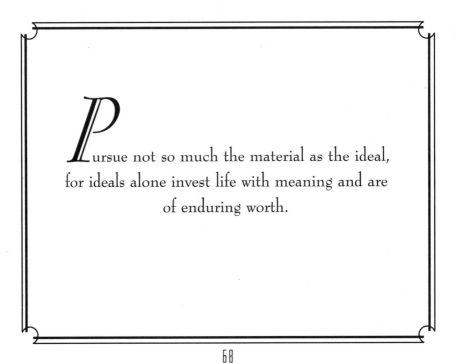

*P*ursue not so much the material as the ideal,
for ideals alone invest life with meaning and are
of enduring worth.

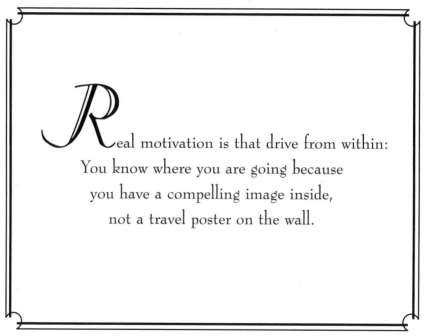

$\mathcal{R}$eal motivation is that drive from within:
You know where you are going because
you have a compelling image inside,
not a travel poster on the wall.

One of the wonderful aspects of the human imagination is its power to break through the barriers of time and space. It can see things not as they are but as they can be.

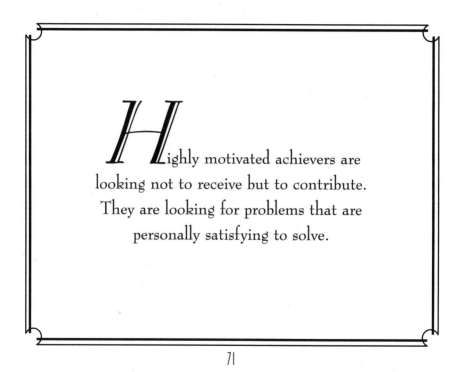

*H*ighly motivated achievers are
looking not to receive but to contribute.
They are looking for problems that are
personally satisfying to solve.

*A*chievers can almost literally taste
success because they imagine their goals in such vivid
detail. Setbacks only seem to add spice and flavor to
the final taste of victory.

Given the chance, a person will create
more exciting and challenging goals for himself or
herself than parents or company managers
could ever dream of.

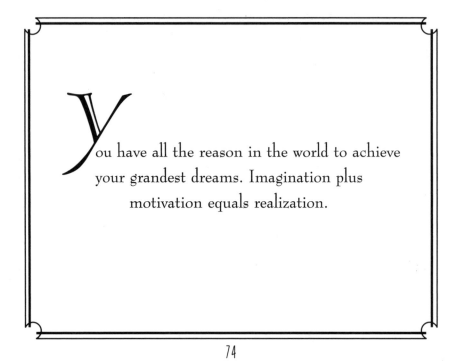

You have all the reason in the world to achieve
your grandest dreams. Imagination plus
motivation equals realization.

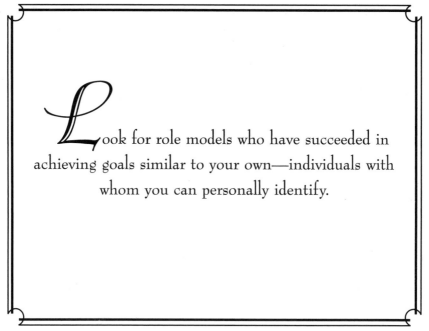

$\mathcal{L}$ook for role models who have succeeded in achieving goals similar to your own—individuals with whom you can personally identify.

$\mathcal{B}$y focusing on positive, healthy motivations and letting the more negative ones pass, you can purify the source of your imaginative power.

*M*ake a list of your current wants and desires. Next to each, put down what benefit or payoff there would be when you achieve it. Look at this list often throughout the day and before retiring at night.

*T*ime and health are two precious assets that we don't recognize and appreciate until they have been depleted.

*F*ind a positive lesson and positive reason for all of your personal relationships. Accentuate the blessings and knowledge gained from each.

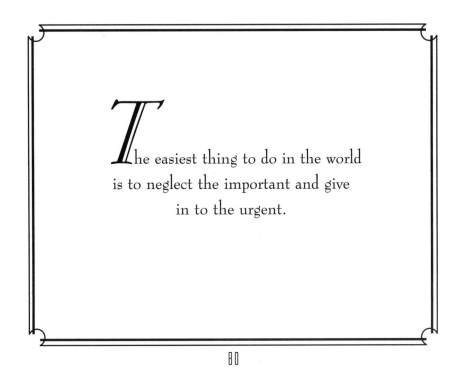

*T*he easiest thing to do in the world
is to neglect the important and give
in to the urgent.

C ourage means to keep working on
a relationship, to continue seeking solutions
to difficult problems, and to stay focused
during stressful periods.

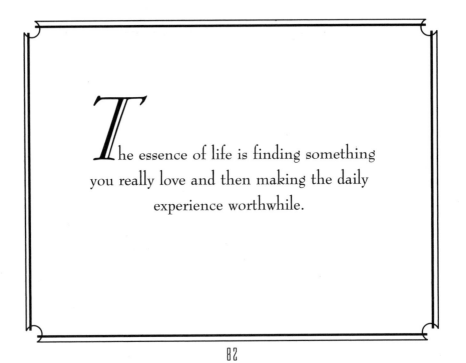

*T*he essence of life is finding something
you really love and then making the daily
experience worthwhile.

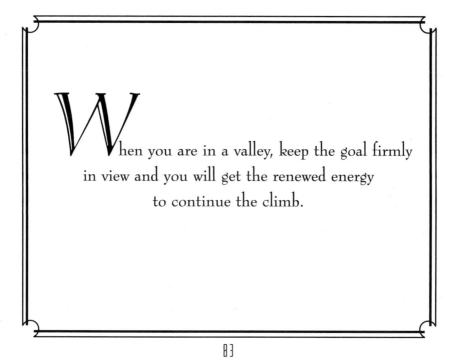

When you are in a valley, keep the goal firmly in view and you will get the renewed energy to continue the climb.

A dream is your creative vision for your life in the future. It is what you would like life to become. A goal is what, specifically, you intend to make happen. Goals should be just out of your present reach, but not out of sight.

No man or woman is an island. To exist just for yourself is meaningless. You can achieve the most satisfaction when you feel related to some greater purpose in life, something greater than yourself.

*F*ailure should be our teacher, not our undertaker. Failure is delay, not defeat. It is a temporary detour, not a dead end. Failure is something we can avoid only by saying nothing, doing nothing, and being nothing.

*I*t is exhilarating to feel in control while operating at the higher limits of your potential. Preparation and reinforcement day by day will be your internal pilot light to keep the spark ignited.

*T*ime changes everything, but with patience we can keep our desires relatively constant. If we can just hang on long enough, time will eventually create for us the conditions in which we can succeed.

*A*s long as we are persistent in our pursuit of our deepest destiny, we will continue to grow. We cannot choose the day or time when we will fully bloom. It happens in its own time.

The patient person accepts a certain amount of failure knowing that it is as important a thread in the fabric of life as is success. Great individuals make great successes out of failure.

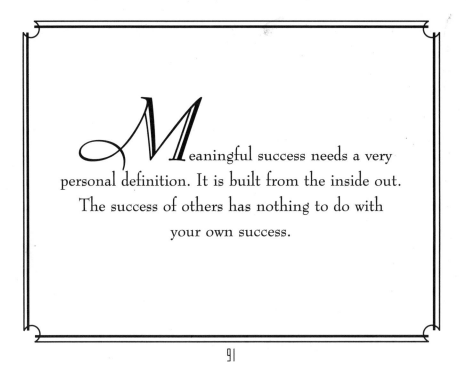

$\mathcal{M}$eaningful success needs a very personal definition. It is built from the inside out. The success of others has nothing to do with your own success.

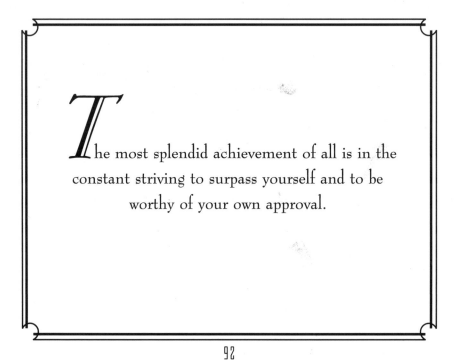

*T*he most splendid achievement of all is in the constant striving to surpass yourself and to be worthy of your own approval.

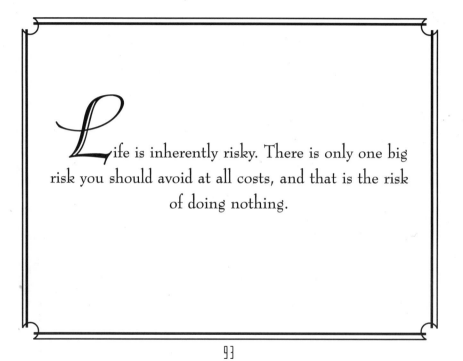

$\mathcal{L}$ife is inherently risky. There is only one big risk you should avoid at all costs, and that is the risk of doing nothing.

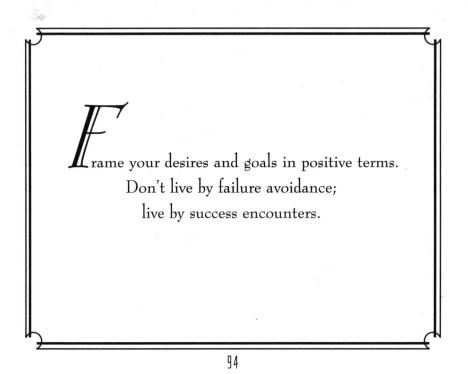

*F*rame your desires and goals in positive terms.
Don't live by failure avoidance;
live by success encounters.

Successful people believe in the validity of their own dreams and goals, even if dreams are all they have to go on.

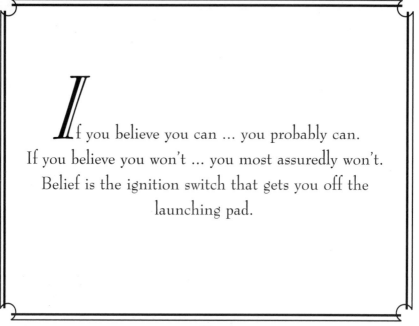

*I*f you believe you can ... you probably can.
If you believe you won't ... you most assuredly won't.
Belief is the ignition switch that gets you off the
launching pad.

Goals provide the energy source that powers our lives. One of the best ways we can get the most from the energy we have is to focus it. That is what goals can do for us: concentrate our energy.

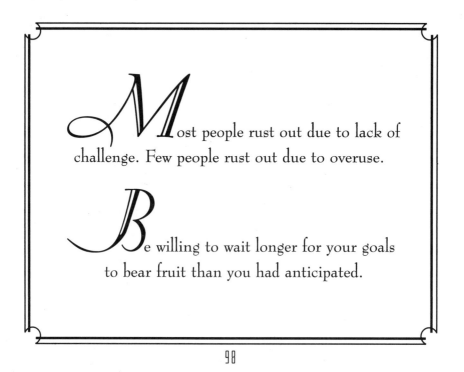

*M*ost people rust out due to lack of
challenge. Few people rust out due to overuse.

*B*e willing to wait longer for your goals
to bear fruit than you had anticipated.

Close your eyes and visualize the person you really want to be, who fits your own concept of self-respect. If you can see the person clearly in the mirror of your mind, you surely will become that person.

$\mathcal{S}$uccess is not a pie with a limited number of pieces. The success of others has very little bearing on your success. You and everyone you know can become successful without anyone suffering setbacks, harm, or downturns.

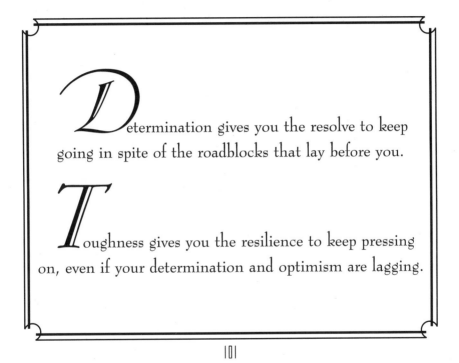

*D*etermination gives you the resolve to keep going in spite of the roadblocks that lay before you.

*T*oughness gives you the resilience to keep pressing on, even if your determination and optimism are lagging.

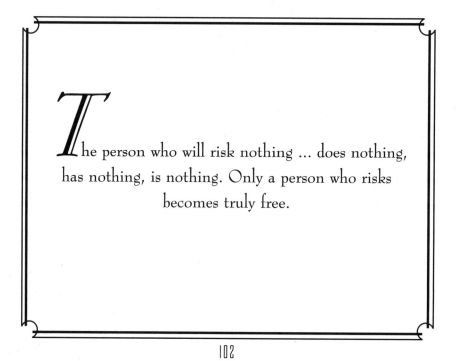

*T*he person who will risk nothing ... does nothing,
has nothing, is nothing. Only a person who risks
becomes truly free.

Only accomplishments that are an expression
of your inner life are richly rewarding to you;
therefore your goals must come from who you are
and what you want.

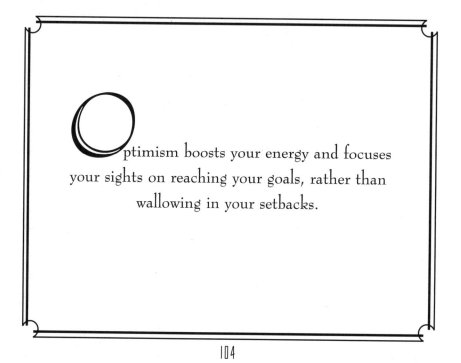

Optimism boosts your energy and focuses
your sights on reaching your goals, rather than
wallowing in your setbacks.

A dream is what you would like your life to become. A goal is what you are truly willing to do to achieve what you really want.

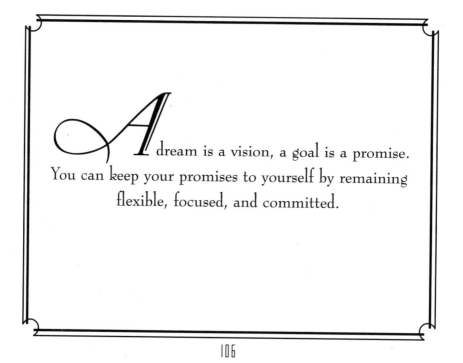

A dream is a vision, a goal is a promise.
You can keep your promises to yourself by remaining
flexible, focused, and committed.

*D*on't wait for mentors to seek you out. Don't ever wait for your phone calls to be returned, your letters to be answered, your faxes to be responded to. Keep going out and asking questions.

*I*t is a psychological fact that we cherish most what we have worked hardest to gain. The further we have come, the sweeter the celebration at the destination when we arrive.

*T*here are two primary choices in life:
to accept conditions as they exist, or
accept the responsibility for changing them.

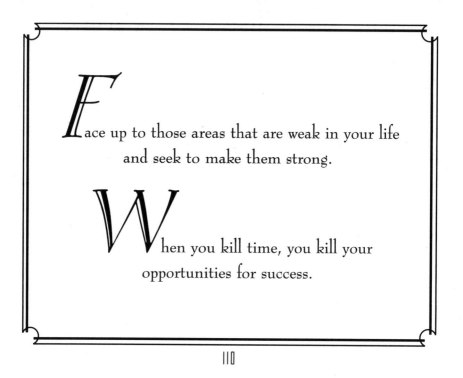

*F*ace up to those areas that are weak in your life
and seek to make them strong.

*W*hen you kill time, you kill your
opportunities for success.

*T*he greatest choice we have is to think before we act and then take action toward our life goals every day. Our problems result not only from our lack of action, but from our action without thought.

Recognize when your peak energy occurs during the day. Allocate the most difficult projects to that period. Work on easy projects at low-energy times.

*T*ime is the most precious element of human existence. The successful person knows how to put energy into time and how to draw success from time.

*I*t is important to remember that the real joy of achievement is in the challenge, not in the accomplishment. In an ever-changing world, the eternal wisdom of the ages never changes: The road to heaven is heaven.

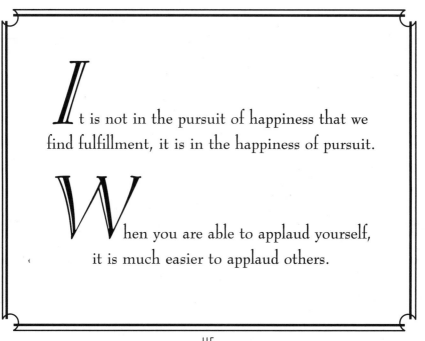

*I*t is not in the pursuit of happiness that we find fulfillment, it is in the happiness of pursuit.

*W*hen you are able to applaud yourself, it is much easier to applaud others.

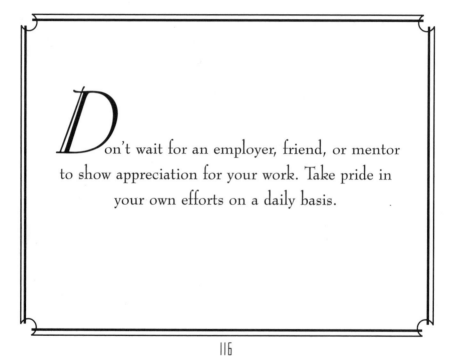

*D*on't wait for an employer, friend, or mentor to show appreciation for your work. Take pride in your own efforts on a daily basis.

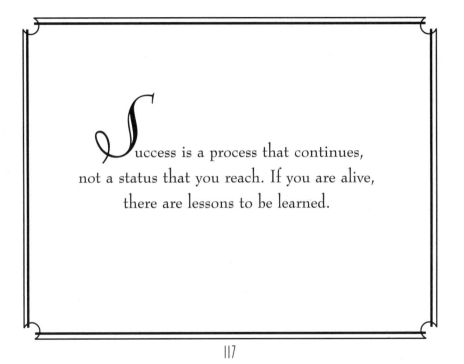

$\mathcal{S}$uccess is a process that continues,
not a status that you reach. If you are alive,
there are lessons to be learned.

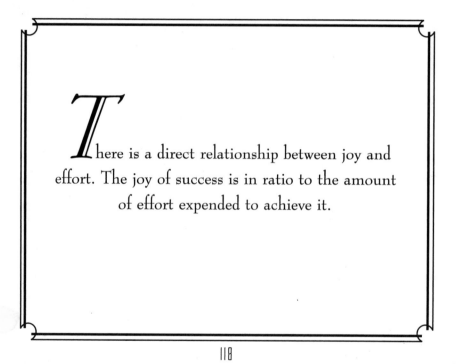

*T*here is a direct relationship between joy and effort. The joy of success is in ratio to the amount of effort expended to achieve it.

$\mathcal{B}$y staying focused and flexible, you will meet and exceed your major life-forming goals. Success is not a resting place—it is a launching pad.

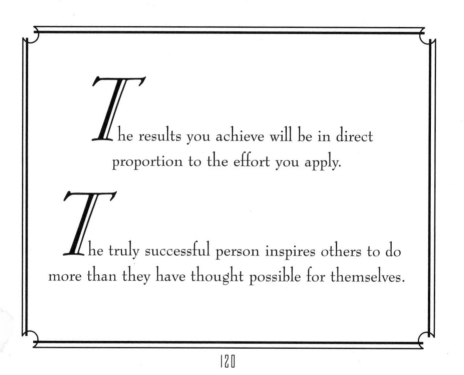

*T*he results you achieve will be in direct
proportion to the effort you apply.

*T*he truly successful person inspires others to do
more than they have thought possible for themselves.

*L*ife is based on growth and finding new challenges to face and overcome, new contributions to make to society, and constantly coming to a better understanding of yourself and the universe in which you live.

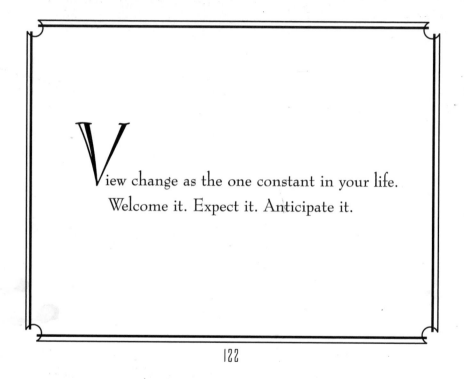

View change as the one constant in your life.
Welcome it. Expect it. Anticipate it.